Body Books

Babies

Anna Sandeman
Illustrated by Ian Thompson

COPPER BEECH BOOKS
BROOKFIELD, CONNECTICUT

Copyright © 1996 Aladdin Books Ltd.
Produced by Aladdin Books Limited
28 Percy Street
London W1P 0LD

First published in the United States in 1996 by
Copper Beech Books,
an imprint of The Millbrook Press
2 Old New Milford Road
Brookfield, Connecticut 06804

Designed by David West Children's Book Design
Designer: Edward Simkins
Photography: Roger Vlitos
Picture Research: Brooks Krikler Research
Consultants: Dr. R. Levene M.D. and Jan Bastoncino, Dip. Ed.

Library of Congress Cataloging-in-Publication Data
Sandeman, Anna.
Babies / by Anna Sandeman;
illustrated by Ian Thompson.
p. cm. – (Body books)
Includes index.
Summary: Looks at the development of a baby both before and
after birth.
ISBN 0-7613-0478-9 (lib. bdg.)
1. Pregnancy–Juvenile literature. 2. Infants–Development–
Juvenile literature. [1. Pregnancy. 2. Babies.] I. Thompson,
Ian, 1964-   . II. Title. III. Series: Sandeman, Anna. Body
books.
QP281.S26 1996   95-40836
612.6–dc20   CIP AC

Printed in Belgium

PHOTO CREDITS
Abbreviations: t-top, m-middle, b-bottom, r-right, l-left
All the pictures in this book were taken by Roger Vlitos
apart from the pictures on the following pages: 6-7m:
Frank Spooner Pictures; 8-9m, 12tl, 12-13m, 13, 14tl,
14-15m, 18t, 29r: Science Photo Library

Contents

Pregnancy   6

Making a baby   8

One baby or two?   10

Starting to grow   12

Getting bigger   14

Family likeness   16

Newborn baby   18

Muscles   20

Senses   22

Body control   24

First words   26

Did you know?   28

Glossary   30

Index   31

Pregnancy

Can you remember being a baby – when you couldn't walk, talk, or even sit up? Doesn't it seem like a long time ago?

Most animals develop and grow much quicker than humans. A lamb or foal struggles to its feet minutes after it has been born. Both are able to look after themselves after only a few weeks. A human baby will probably not walk without help until after its first birthday and is not expected to take care of itself for at least 16 years.

Even before birth, a human baby takes much longer to develop than most other animal babies. A human mother is pregnant for nine months. A mouse gives birth after 20 days, a cat after nine weeks. The populations of these animals can increase quickly. Only large animals, such as the whale or the elephant, are pregnant for longer – the first for twelve months, the second for 22 months.

Making a baby

A woman becomes pregnant when a tiny part of a man, called a sperm, joins with a minute egg inside her body.

Sperm are made inside a man's testes. You cannot see sperm without a microscope but they look like tadpoles. Each has a head and a long tail. They swim in a sticky liquid called semen.

When a man and a woman want to show their love for each other, the man's penis becomes hard so that it can enter an opening in the woman's body, called the vagina.

Sperm and semen are then squirted through the man's penis into the vagina. From here the sperm swim upward in their search for an egg.

Here, many sperm are trying to penetrate an egg. Only one will succeed.

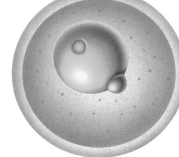

Close-up of the inside of a woman's egg

One baby or two?

A woman's eggs are stored in her ovaries. Every month an egg leaves an ovary to travel down one of two fallopian tubes leading to the uterus. If it meets and joins with a sperm, the egg is fertilized. The fertilized egg is now an embryo. This is the beginning of the baby that will be born nine months later.

A fertilized egg splits into two cells. These two cells divide again and again to form a ball of cells. The ball of cells travels on to the uterus where it settles into the soft lining.

A fertilized egg divides to form one baby.

Egg is fertilized by a sperm

Ovary

Embryo embeds

Vagina

Non-identical twins form when two eggs are fertilized.

Uterus

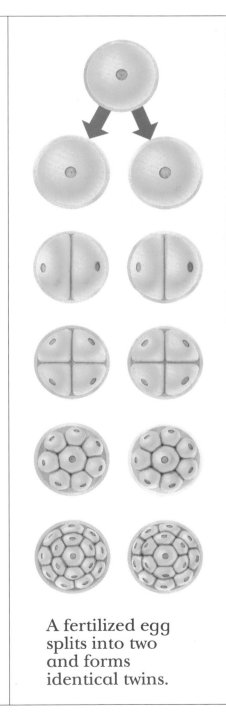

If two eggs are fertilized, the babies will be non-identical twins. They may look different from each other and be different sexes.

Sometimes a fertilized egg splits into two separate halves. Each half then grows into a baby. These will be identical twins. They will be either boys or girls.

A fertilized egg splits into two and forms identical twins.

Starting to grow

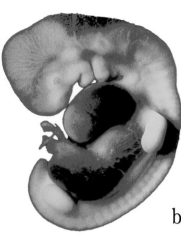

An embryo at 30 days

Inside the uterus, the cells grow rapidly. They quickly begin to take the shape of a head and back bone. By day 25 the heart is beating, even though the baby is only a quarter inch long – about the size of a baked bean.

By week eight, the baby is one inch long. Although it is small it already has arms, legs, fingers, and toes. It also has the beginnings of a mouth and a nose.

An embryo at eight weeks

The baby lives inside a kind of bag filled with liquid. This protects the baby against any bumps and keeps the baby from becoming too hot or too cold.

The baby is fed by its mother. The food comes in tiny particles, called nutrients. These pass from the mother's blood into a tube, called the umbilical cord, and then into the baby. Look at your belly button and you will see where your umbilical cord once grew. After birth, the baby no longer needs its umbilical cord so it dries up and drops off.

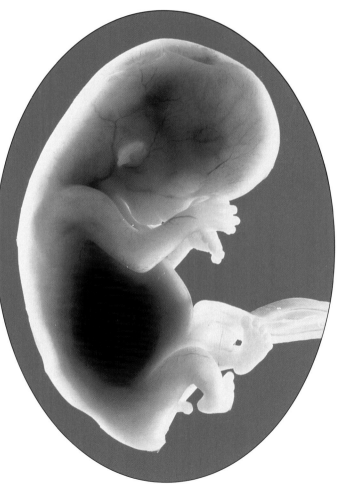

An embryo at eleven weeks

Getting bigger

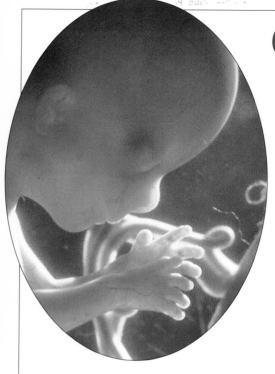

At 16 weeks the baby is about five inches long and weighs about two ounces. It has developed eyes, ears, a nose, and a mouth as well as finger and toe nails. At this stage the baby grows quickly and the mother's belly is getting larger.

An embryo at 20 weeks

The embryo at 16 weeks is developing rapidly.

At 20 weeks the mother can feel the baby kicking as it grows and its muscles get stronger. The baby can hear, swallow, and suck its thumb. It is beginning to recognize its mother's voice. Some babies even get hiccups!

At 28 weeks the baby is about 14 inches (30 cm) long. It weighs about 32 ounces, still less than half the weight it will be at birth. Soon the baby will turn around so that its head is facing downward. It is getting ready to be born.

At 36 weeks the baby's lungs are fully formed. If it were born now, it would be able to breathe on its own. The baby continues to put on weight. By the time it is born at around 40 weeks it will be about 20 inches (50 cm) long and weigh about seven pounds (3.5 kg).

Family likeness

When a baby is born, friends and relatives often say that it looks like its mom or dad. Why?

Both the sperm from the dad, and the egg from the mom, which join up to start a baby, carry their own kind of body pattern. When the egg is fertilized, the two patterns mix together to make a new pattern. This new pattern becomes the body plan for the baby.

Look at this photo of an eight-year-old and his parents. Who does the boy look more like?

The patterns that a mother and father pass on to their baby are made up of the patterns given to them by their own parents. This means that a baby may also look a little like its grandparents.

Ask if you can use photos of your family to make a family tree. Look at eyes, noses, and mouths to see which are most like yours. Look at your brothers and sisters too. How are they like you?

Newborn baby

A baby grows most quickly before it is born. After birth, growth is slower. By the end of its first year, it is about three times its birth weight.

As a baby grows, it changes shape. A newborn baby looks very different from you. Although its head is big – about a quarter the length of its body – its arms reach down only to its hips. Measure the length of your head and arms compared with the rest of you.

Four months

One year

Three years

Look at the pictures below to see how a child's body changes between birth and the age of twelve. What do you notice?

Six years

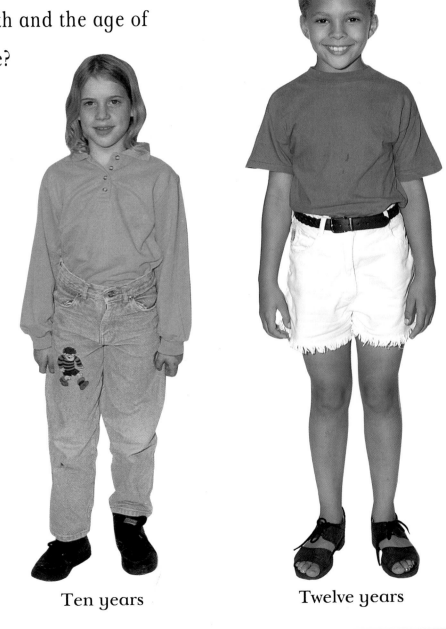

Ten years

Twelve years

Muscles

Unlike most animals, a newborn baby is almost completely helpless. It can't walk, talk, sit, or even lift its head. Its muscles are too weak. Almost all it can do is cry – very loudly.

But from the moment of birth, a baby starts exercising. It waves its arms about and kicks its legs to make its muscles stronger. At this stage, the baby has no control over its movements so it may hit itself in the face by mistake.

Gradually babies learn to use other muscles. By the age of three months, most babies are trying to prop themselves up on their forearms.

By the age of five or six months most babies can hold their heads up and can sit up with some help.

By eight months, they can sit up without help. At nine months, most babies have learned to crawl.

By eleven months they can walk upright if someone holds their hands, and by their first birthday they may have taken their first step alone.

Senses

Although newborn babies can't move much, they can see, hear, taste, smell, and feel things around them.

At first babies can only see things clearly that are very close. When a baby is four weeks old, it watches its mother's face closely as she speaks.

Even very young babies are startled by sudden loud noises. They may blink, cry, fling their arms up, or lie quiet.

Babies are soothed by soft rhythmic sounds. Lullabies, or even a ticking clock may send them to sleep.

Babies have a strong sense of taste and can suck very hard. At first they live just on milk, which they suck from their mother or from a bottle. When they are between three and six months old, they are usually given their first solid food. Most babies quickly make it clear which foods they like and which they don't.

Babies have a sense of smell, too. They even recognize their mothers by their smell.

Crying babies often calm down if they are picked up and cuddled.

Body control

Slowly babies learn to control different parts of their body. At three months of age, they can hold a rattle for a few seconds. At five months, they can grab a nearby toy with two hands. At six or seven months, they can feed themselves a cracker and help to hold a spoon while eating. They now reach for a toy with one hand.

A month or two later, most babies can hold a toy block in each hand. They turn the blocks around to feel their shape and enjoy banging them on the table.

At ten months, they can bring their thumb and finger together to pick up much smaller objects, such as a piece of string or a pea, and move them carefully from one place to another.

By 18 months they will usually have learned to pile blocks on top of each other or to push objects along the floor with their hands.

Waah

First words If you

couldn't talk or write, how would you make people understand you? Try asking for a cracker without saying anything. How long does it take to get the cracker?

Doggie

Small babies have to make themselves understood by crying. They have different cries for when they are hungry, tired, wet, or in pain.

Babies coo, gurgle, and babble. The baby hears people talking and tries to imitate what is being said.

Toward the end of a baby's first year, a baby often says its first real words, such as Mommy, cup, or spoon. In its second year, the baby starts to add words to these names – for example, "Where Teddy?" "Nice doggie."

By the beginning of their third year most babies know enough words to make themselves understood. They can walk and are getting better at making their bodies do what they want. Some are even out of diapers! They are no longer babies; they have become toddlers.

Did you know?

...that a newborn baby's brain is one quarter the weight of an adult's brain, even though an adult is twenty times heavier than a baby?

...that a woman in Russia gave birth to a total of 69 children? She had 16 pairs of twins, seven sets of triplets, and four sets of quadruplets.

...that more boys are born than girls? Most babies are born between April and July.

...that if you hold a newborn baby upright, with its feet on the floor, it will try to take steps?

...that a baby has about 350 bones in its body – that's about 140 more than a grown-up?

...that a woman's egg is smaller than a period?

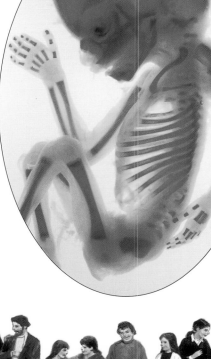

Glossary

Egg – The female sex cell produced by the ovaries

Ovaries – The female organs that produce eggs

Fertilization – The process by which a female egg and male sperm join to develop into a new baby

Pregnancy –The development of a baby inside the uterus

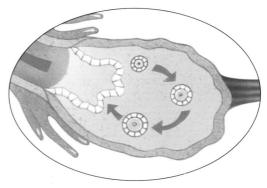

Sperm – The male sex cell produced by the testes

Uterus – The female organ in which the baby develops until it is born

Index

babbling 26

crying 20, 23, 26

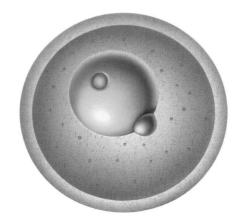

egg 8, 9, 10, 11, 16, 29, 30

embryo 10

fallopian tube 10

fertilization 8, 10, 11, 16, 30

identical twins 11

non-identical twins 11

ovary 10, 30

pregnancy 6, 7, 8, 30

semen 8, 9

sperm 8, 9, 10, 16, 30

testes 8, 30

toddlers 27

umbilical cord 13

uterus 10, 11, 12, 30